# A MAN AND HIS ETHICS

## JOHN GREENING

REGULAR BAPTIST
RBP Press

*A Man and His Ethics*
© 2007
Regular Baptist Press • Arlington Heights, Illinois
www.RegularBaptistPress.org • 1-800-727-4440
Printed in U.S.A.
All rights reserved
RBP5344 • ISBN 978-1-59402-332-3

Third Printing—2019

# CONTENTS

# PREFACE

WHAT do you think God had in mind when He called believers to "be holy, for I am holy" (1 Peter 1:16)? When you hear the word "holy," you might picture a shaft of light coming from Heaven and shining down on a man with a halo who is kneeling to pray. While an artist might render holiness in this way, it doesn't convey the extent to which God defines holiness. In 1 Peter 1:14–16 Peter framed the concept of holiness in terms of a believer's everyday behavior: "As obedient children, not conforming yourselves to the former lusts, as in your ignorance; but as He who called you is holy, you also be holy in all your conduct, because it is written, 'Be holy, for I am holy.'"

God cares about your conduct—all of your conduct. He wants you to respond in every situation in a way that is totally consistent with how He would respond. To act in that holy manner requires that you know God's behavioral standards. Acquiring that knowledge requires a careful consideration of the subject of this study, *A Man and His Ethics*.

The intent of this book is to help you begin a quest to be the man God intended when He made you and saved you. By your every action He wants you to show that your life is controlled and empowered by the holy God of the Bible. May God's grace enable you to live a holy life.

# 1

# WHO WRITES THE RULES?

*God, the Ultimate Authority, has
established rules we must obey.*

D URING a creative moment, my son and I set out to
see if we could invent a table game. It was a challenging project. First we had to come up with a concept.
Then we needed to establish rules for the game. If we didn't
have a set of rules, we couldn't play the game, and we wouldn't
have any sense of how to play or how to declare a winner. The
game play would go nowhere and make no sense.

1. Give an example from each of the following settings in
   which a clearly defined set of rules is required. In contrast, describe what might occur in each of the examples if rules were ignored.

| Setting | Rules | Consequence of Ignoring Rules |
|---|---|---|
| Sports | | |
| Community | | |
| School | | |
| Workplace | | |

## Living by the Rules

The sports field, the highways, the hallways, and the office would be utter chaos without rules. For any cooperative activity to take place with a semblance of order, it must have rules.

2. What statement in Judges 21:25 describes a society that refused to function by a governing set of rules?

Judges 21:25 implies that if a king had been appointed, the anarchy might have been avoided. As the designated leader, a king would have established and enforced a set of rules. A synonym for "king" is "ruler." To rule is to exercise authority, to govern, and to authoritatively lay down a legal rule.

3. For any given day, list your activities that are governed by rules.

Whether or not you like rules, they are an essential part of your life. Rules are designed to provide behavioral parameters within which you function. They enable people to live, work, drive, and play together. Rules regulate acceptable and unacceptable conduct. Their existence implies that right and wrong behavior can be and should be defined.

What rules govern your conduct? The collective answer to that question could be described as a man and his ethics. Ethics is a system of moral principles that governs an individual's or a group's behavior. As with rules, ethics assumes the existence of an authority who determines right and wrong.

4. What authorities establish a person's code of conduct?

The existence of ethics implies that a person decides either to live by set standards or to refuse to accept them. As you think about ethics, consider three questions: Who establishes your ethics? What are those ethics? Do you and will you live by those ethics?

## Ethical Authority

The starting point for a study of ethics is to determine their origin. Who sets the rules? Perhaps you remember when you were growing up and your parents made a rule such as, "You can't go out with your friends unless your homework is finished and your room is clean." How would your parents have responded if you had snapped back, "What right do you have to make that rule for me?" Probably the response would have been, "Because I'm the parent and you are the child. I'm in charge, not you. You will do what you are told, young man." Chances are that you would not have been able to go out with friends after responding in that smart-aleck manner.

What response would you expect if you were a member of

an athletic team and the coach said, "I want you to run wind sprints before you leave practice," but you refused his instructions? You would have been running more than the required wind sprints or possibly would have been dismissed from the team. It is assumed that you, as a team member, would do what you were told because the coach was in charge.

The Bible contains ethical guidelines for conduct. They are intended to govern your behavior in areas such as marriage and family, friendships, finances, worship, and speech. You may or may not like those guidelines. The question is, who is in charge and has the right to impose those rules? The answer is found in the opening chapters of the Bible.

Read Genesis 1.

5. What laws of nature apply to the natural creation (Genesis 1:1–25)?

6. What laws of nature apply to man (Genesis 1:26–30)?

7. Who established those laws of nature? What authority does He have that entitles Him to make those laws?

Read Genesis 2.

8. What rule applied to the natural creation, as recorded in Genesis 2:4–6?

9. What guidelines for right and wrong behavior existed in the Garden (Genesis 2:7–25)?

10. Who established those guidelines? What authority does He have that entitles Him to set those guidelines?

The opening chapters of the Bible are essential to understanding the origin of the universe and the origin of ethics. The Creator God made everything that exists. By right of His creative act, His authority also extends over man, who likewise finds his origin in God. If God made everything that exists, including man, then He is entitled to set the rules by which it all functions.

11. Do you agree with that reasoning? Why or why not?

When God made the first man, Adam, He gave him specific duties. He established a rule about what Adam should and should not eat. When God made Eve and brought her to Adam, immediately Adam realized a sense of divinely arranged compatibility and responsibility. God not only made Adam and Eve, but He also established a basic order by which they were to live. God had every right to do that because He had created them.

Think back to the time when you were a child at home with your parents. Your parents had authority to set the rules in your family because they had produced you and you were living in their house. You belonged to them. Even more so, the human race finds its origin in God. The universe is His house. Everything belongs to Him. He made it and He made you. As long as you are living in His house, you are responsible to live by His rules.

## Overthrowing Ethical Authority

A coup d'etat is the coordinated overthrow of an existing governing power and the institution of a new authority. Occasionally the news will report that a coup d'etat has taken place in a nation; a new regime forcefully replaces the reigning leader. A similar type of coup takes place when you replace God as the ethical authority of your life.

12. How would a man's ethics be affected if he decided that the God of Genesis 1 and 2 did not make the universe?

Read Romans 1:18–32.

13. What decision did men make regarding God's authority (Romans 1:18–23)?

14. Who was appointed as the new ethical authority (Romans 1:24, 25)?

15. What behavioral standards did man accept (Romans 1:28–32)?

16.  How did these behavioral standards disregard the rules of nature that God instituted in the original creation order (Romans 1:26, 27)?

17.  What impact would the new behavioral standards have on families, businesses, neighborhoods, and nations (Romans 1:29–31)?

18.  What summary statement defines the attitude of sinful man toward God's ethical authority (Romans 1:32)?

19.  Does this description of man's ethical choices sound familiar to you? From current events, provide illustrations of these behavioral choices.

20.  Have you acknowledged God's authority over your life? What personal evidence can you give of God's authority in your life?

When man initiated a new set of ethical principles (Romans 1), he rewrote God's ethics. Man appointed himself as the authority, seizing the right to devise his own rules in defiant protest to God's ethics.

## Inward look

During your life you periodically receive personal assessments: doctors assess your health; teachers assess your academic success; employers assess your job performance. Ideally the intent of these assessments is to reveal strengths and weaknesses. If God assessed your response to His moral authority, how would you score?

21. Conduct a personal assessment by placing an X on the continuum after each of the following assessments.

**I accept God as my ultimate ethical authority.**

Reject                                                      Accept

**I have a thorough knowledge of God's ethical absolutes.**

Unaware                                                      Aware

**My conduct evidences a consistent compliance to God's ethical expectations.**

Defiant                                                      Compliant

22. How did you rank in response to God's standard of ethics? List specific areas in which you could improve in your awareness of and compliance to God's ethical absolutes.

Ask the Lord to use this study as an ethical assessment of your life. Ask God to show you areas of moral strength and weakness and to help you take the necessary steps to live consistently by His ethical guidelines.

# 2

# COUNTING THE CONSEQUENCES

*The consequences of sin affect our*
*everyday lives.*

IMAGINE a man you never met before walking into your home. Shortly after he arrives he begins to reposition your furniture. He tells you he likes the new placement better than your arrangement. He proceeds to your kitchen where your wife is preparing your favorite dinner. He questions her cooking procedures and menu. He tells her that he doesn't care for her menu, and then he recommends something more to his liking. He even explains how he would prepare the food. Alarmingly, your wife goes along with the new menu. A little later you overhear this man in the backyard telling your kids how to behave. The conduct he suggests is contrary to the guidelines you've established. To your amazement you observe your children following the stranger's suggestions. Later when you are alone with your wife, she tells you that she was impressed with the man. She exclaims, "What he said and did made sense!" How would you react?

As strange as that scenario seems, something similar happened in the opening chapters of the Bible.

## An Uninvited Intruder

1. Read Genesis 3:1–6. Who are the participants in this account?

2. To whom did the Garden ultimately belong (Genesis 2:8)?

3. Who originally established the duties and moral boundary for the caretakers of the Garden (Genesis 1:26–30; 2:15–17)?

4. What were those duties and moral boundary (Genesis 1:26–30; 2:15–17)?

5. What did the serpent propose regarding the moral boundary (Genesis 3:4, 5)?

6. How did Adam and Eve respond to the serpent's proposal (Genesis 3:6)?

What a startling turn of events! The serpent (Satan) came into God's house, questioned God's moral authority, and then proposed rewriting God's rule. Rather than telling the serpent to mind his own business and depart, the man and the woman chose to follow the serpent's proposed new moral guideline. Imagine the audacity of the serpent, challenging the moral authority of the Creator. Imagine the arrogance of the serpent, proposing to rewrite God's moral guideline. Imagine the foolishness of the man and the woman in choosing to follow the serpent's suggestion and in defying the moral boundary imposed by their Creator.

7. What had God previously told Adam and Eve would be the consequence for violating His moral guideline regarding the tree (Genesis 2:15–17)?

8. What did Adam and Eve's moral choice cause them to experience toward each other (Genesis 3:7)? Compare with Genesis 2:25.

9. What did Adam and Eve's moral choice cause them to experience toward God (Genesis 3:8–10)?

10. What did Adam and Eve's moral choice cause them to do when confronted by God about their actions (Genesis 3:11–13)?

## Making a Mess of Things

The innocence, openness, and harmony of moral purity
that had existed among the first man, his wife, and God were
horribly corrupted. Innocence was replaced by shame and
guilt. Openness was supplanted by concealment and fear. Harmony was substituted by faultfinding and excuse-making. This
fallout was the result of the man and his wife's making the
wrong moral choice.

11. What consequences did God pronounce on each of the
    following for violating His moral guidelines?
    (a) Serpent (Genesis 3:14, 15)


    (b) Eve (Genesis 3:16)


    (c) Adam (Genesis 3:17–19)


    (d) Mankind (Romans 5:12–14)


The simplicity and pleasure of living by God's rules gave
way to a hellish nightmare of sweat, pain, heartache, estrange-
ment, and death after Adam and Eve violated God's boundary. Bad moral choices resulted in negative consequences.
God says defiance of His ethics is sin. Sin leaves its scars.

12. According to God, what moral capacity did man ac-
    quire as a result of defying God's moral authority and
    eating the forbidden fruit (Genesis 3:22)?

13. What are the negative implications for society because people possess this moral capacity?

### Trouble at Home

God repeatedly described His creation as "good" (Genesis 1:10, 12, 18, 21, 25); this positive assessment included man (Genesis 1:31). Tragically that description changed when Adam and Eve acquiesced to the enticement of Satan. From that point on, the moral pollution of evil was present within creation and within man himself. Evil began to express itself in man's thoughts and actions.

14. What morally evil attitude did Adam and Eve's son Cain exhibit when he realized that God did not respect his sacrifice (Genesis 4:3–5)?

15. To whom was that attitude directed, and why was that attitude evil?

16. Has that morally evil attitude ever been present in your life? Describe the situation.

17. Why do you think God confronted Cain about his moral condition (Genesis 4:6)?

18. Have you ever been confronted about evil in your life? Describe the occasion. How did you feel about that confrontation? What moral choice did you make?

19. What moral options did God explain to Cain (Genesis 4:7)?

20. What evil moral action did Cain take against Abel (Genesis 4:8)?

21. How did Cain react when God questioned him about his brother's whereabouts (Genesis 4:9), and what lack of moral integrity did Cain's answer reveal?

22. What consequences did Cain experience for his moral choices (Genesis 4:10–16)?

The choices of Cain and Abel represent the bottom-line issue that every man must address regarding morality. There is a good or right way, which is established by God. Conversely, there is an evil or wrong way that is counter to God's established way. Will you choose the right way or the wrong way as the governing moral guide for your life?

## Decision Time

Draw a stick figure of a man standing at a fork in the road. Label one road "God's way—good morals," and label the other road, "Alternative way—evil morals."

Now write your own name over the man on your drawing. Fix this picture in your mind. It portrays the moral choices you must make throughout the day: God's way of good morals or the alternative way of evil morals?

## In Deep Water

Read Genesis 6:1–13.

23. What was God's assessment of man's moral intentions and choices (Genesis 6:5)?

24. Contrast the moral conduct of Noah and humanity by listing the descriptive words for each (Genesis 6:8–13).
    (a)  Noah

    (b)  Humanity

25. How did God react to humanity's moral condition (Genesis 6:6, 7, 13)?

26. What consequence did humanity experience for not living within God's moral boundaries (Genesis 7:4)?

27. How did God react to Noah's moral conduct (Genesis 6:8, 9), and what was the benefit Noah experienced for living within God's moral boundaries (Genesis 7:23)?

As unflattering as it may be, each man must face his own moral condition. The consequences of Adam's act of defiance against God's rules have touched every person from that time forward, leaving humanity in moral crisis (Romans 5:12–14).

28. Read Romans 3:9–18 to gain an appraisal of man's moral condition. Write a summary statement of this description in your own words, using the personal pronoun *I*.

You are in moral crisis apart from God. Like Noah, you need a means of rescue from the consequences of sin. Read Romans 3:21–26 to discover the deliverance from sin's consequences that is possible through faith in Jesus Christ. Through His death and His shed blood, your sins are forgiven. Have you ever trusted Jesus Christ as the only means by which you may be rescued from the consequences of your sin? If not, acknowledge your sin to God and believe that He can save you. Accept Him now by faith and you will be saved.

# 3

## MEN BEHAVING BADLY

*Rebellion against God is a choice—*
*one we face every day.*

WHETHER you realize it or not, a set of ethical standards guides your life. It influences the decision-making process that continually operates within you, directing your thoughts, words, and behavior. This set of ethical standards comes from your life experiences as well as from your God-given sense of morality.

Think for a moment about the code of morality by which you live. Several outside factors have been influencing you. They have come from people such as your parents, family members, schoolteachers, pastors, Sunday School teachers, and friends and from things such as music, television, books, and laws. Each of these influences espouses a particular view of right and wrong.

Within you exists another significant moral influence. You have an instinctive sense of moral right and wrong that comes directly from God. The Bible suggests that Gentiles (non-

Jews), who did not receive the law of God as did the Jews, were still responsible to God because they had the work of the law written on their hearts (Romans 2:12–16). All of mankind possesses this inherent moral code. Some individuals choose to ignore this code; others choose to heed it.

To understand the moral decision-making process, picture in your mind a committee meeting taking place. The members are addressing the topic of morality. Sitting around a table are people in your life who influence your morality. The task of the committee is to make recommendations on how you should respond to a given situation. Each member shares an opinion. Depending on the weight of the situation you are facing, particular members argue strongly for their point of view. In the end, you must decide which member's advice to follow.

As you choose the advice to follow, your spiritual condition has a bearing on your moral decision making. Have you considered your spiritual life lately? Do you have a relationship with God through faith in Jesus Christ? If so, do you allow the Holy Spirit Who dwells within you to achieve His purpose in your life? Or are you hindering the Holy Spirit's work because of sin you are harboring?

Though an unsaved person may make a moral decision that is consistent with God's guidelines, this person's choice does not win him merit with God. The Bible explains that good works are not the means by which people are saved (Ephesians 2:8, 9). It is only through faith in God's gracious act of forgiveness, extended through Christ's sacrifice for your sins, that you can be saved. Have you trusted Christ as your Savior? If not, believe on Him now and you will be saved. By doing so, you can begin a new life, empowered by God to live in a manner that is pleasing to Him.

God's desire is that you give the greatest weight to His view of right and wrong when choosing your thoughts, words, and actions. God has made His view of morality known in the Bible. We must be diligent students of the Bible if we are to understand right and wrong from God's perspective. The following three Biblical accounts offer lessons from which you can learn about God's moral guidelines.

## Family Choices

Genesis 8:20–22 records Noah's actions after the world-wide flood. When the flood waters subsided, Noah constructed an altar on which he offered a burnt offering to the Lord. The Lord was pleased with Noah's expression of worship. He assured Noah that He would never again curse the ground or destroy all living things as He had done by that flood. God gave Noah a rainbow as a sign to remind him and subsequent generations that God would honor His promise.

1. What moral capacity of man did God acknowledge (Genesis 8:21)?

2. What moral commands did God institute (Genesis 9:1–7)?

God was well aware of the potential that man possessed for thinking and doing evil. It was necessary for God to create moral boundaries within which He expected man to live.

3. As a result of your study of the moral guidance God communicated to Noah and his family (Genesis 9:1–7), what ethical questions are raised for the following areas of life?

(a)  Family (v. 1)

(b)  Animals (vv. 2, 3)

(c)  Diet (vv. 3, 4)

(d)  Dignity of human life (vv. 5, 6)

God wants you to think carefully about your actions in each
of these areas. The entire Bible must be considered to determine the proper moral decisions God wants you to make. The
intent of this study is not to address the specifics of these areas
but to illustrate the need to use the Word to discover God's ethics by which you are to live. Unfortunately, mankind has repeatedly chosen not to follow God's ethical standards.

4.  How has mankind shifted away from God's moral
guidelines in these areas?
(a)  Family (1 Timothy 4:1–3; Romans 1:26, 27)

(b)  Animals (Romans 1:21–23)

(c)  Diet (1 Timothy 4:3–5)

(d)  Dignity of human life (James 4:1, 2)


God used an unflattering experience from Noah's life to provide moral guidance and to highlight the consequences of not following God's standards.

Read Genesis 9:20–27.

5.  What did Noah do as a result of his drunkenness?


6.  What can drunkenness cause people to do?


Though specifics are not included in this account, it states that Noah drank enough wine to become drunk. Ham found his father lying naked in a drunken stupor. Rather than covering his father, Ham looked upon him and must have entertained an inappropriate thought. He left the tent where his father lay exposed and shared the information with his brothers, possibly thinking they might be interested in the sordid details. In contrast to Ham, his brothers responded differently by acting discreetly and modestly in covering their father.

7.  What were the consequences or blessings that resulted from their moral choices (Genesis 9:24–27)?


8.  What influence can a father's drunkenness have on his family?

9. Based on the experience of Noah, what would be the wisest course of action for you to take toward alcoholic beverages?

As stated in Genesis 8:21, man's heart has the capacity to generate evil thoughts and actions. In regard to sin, you are not an island to yourself. Your actions affect others' lives.

10. Name the people who are impacted by your actions, whether good or bad.

11. When faced with making a moral decision, how should thoughts of friends, coworkers, or family influence your course of action?

At the beginning of Genesis 9, Noah stood united with his sons as God conveyed to them His moral expectations. The Bible account is a touching scene of a family considering the morals by which they will live. They had just come through the remarkable experience of God's delivering them from the Flood. Through that flood experience God recognized Noah as a man of faith to whom He extended His favor. However the account later depicts a quite different scene of a family damaged and divided due to their poor moral choices. Don't make the mistake of violating God's moral standards. The tragic consequences will produce only pain and shame.

## Trouble at the Tower

As the human population of the earth began to grow after the Flood, the nomadic people found a pleasant place to live in an area called Shinar.

12. What did the people propose to build (Genesis 11:1–4)?


13. What was the reason for proposing that colossal construction project (Genesis 11:4)?


14. How did this plan violate the responsibility God had given man to "fill the earth" (Genesis 1:28; 9:1)?


15. How did God react to the plan (Genesis 11:5–9)?


16. What threat did that cooperative project pose from God's perspective (Genesis 11:6)?


The potential one person has for devising evil out of his heart is compounded when people put their minds together. The tower of Babel was not simply an attempt at architectural achievement; it was a self-promoting effort launched by man to displace God as the authority. God knew that if He permitted man to continue devising his own plans, the human race would be acting as it had prior to the Flood—concocting and carrying out all kinds of evil.

17. What did the poor moral choices of the people of Babel cost them in terms of the unity they had hoped to achieve (Genesis 11:6–9)?

The track record of sin shows that it does not bring people together. Sin divides people, often resulting in bitter disputes.

18. What examples from families or current events demonstrate that poor moral choices divide rather than unite people?

## A Legacy of Faith and Failure

The book of Genesis contains the account of the family of Jews that became the focus of God's special attention. The founding father of this family was Abraham. The life accounts of Abraham's descendants are recorded in Genesis. These accounts offer many lessons related to the study of morals. The Bible is a candid presentation of the moral strengths and weaknesses of great heroes of the faith.

Read Genesis 12:10–20.

19. What scheme did Abram devise in an attempt to protect himself (Genesis 12:10–13)?

20. What moral decisions of right or wrong did Abram make (Genesis 12:10–16)?

21. What consequence occurred in Pharaoh's household as a result of Abram's decision (Genesis 12:17–20)?

22. What was Pharaoh's moral code in regard to a man's word (Genesis 12:18–20)?

23. What action did Pharaoh take when he learned the truth about Abram's wife, Sarai (Genesis 12:19, 20)?

24. What recurring problem regarding truthfulness occurred in Genesis 20?

25. What pattern of untruthfulness surfaced in Abraham's family and descendants?
    (a) Sarah, Abraham's wife (Genesis 18:10–15)

    (b) Isaac, Abraham's son (Genesis 26:6–10)

   (c)  Jacob, Abraham's grandson (Genesis 27)

   (d)  Laban, Abraham's grandson's uncle (Genesis 29:1–30)

   (e)  Joseph's brothers, Abraham's great grandsons (Genesis 37:12–36)

26. What does this account teach about the importance of truthfulness?

    Honesty is the best policy. By living according to God's moral guidelines, you can't lose. His way is always best. The consequences of violating God's moral guidelines have far-reaching effects. Every day you make moral judgments. When the morals committee meets in your heart and each member shares an opinion, make sure the voice you listen to is God's, as communicated in His Word.

    The Bible presents the good and bad of life. A wise man will learn not only from his own failures but also from those of others. Pause and ask God to help you face your moral failures. He wants you to learn to make decisions according to His standards.

# 4

# HERE ARE
# THE RULES

*God laid down the rules for morality,*
*starting with putting Him first.*

I'M FEELING a bit sick: I just read in the newspaper's sports section that the quarterback for my favorite college football team won't be playing in a bowl game this year. The news account states that the young man was suspended for violating the team and NCAA rules. The infraction will cost him a trip to his first bowl game as a starter and may affect the team's play. To his credit, the star athlete had the courage to acknowledge his actions. In a statement released to the media he admitted, "I am aware of what is expected . . . , and I have fallen short of those expectations."

A good coach cares about not only the physical conditioning and athletic skills of his team members, but also about their conduct. He knows that behavior affects the morale, harmony, and ultimately the success of the team. At the beginning of the season, coaches typically hold a mandatory player-orientation session. In that session the coach spells out the team rules. It becomes the responsibility of each athlete to abide by those rules. If a player does not follow the rules, he must suffer the consequences. The quarterback of my favorite team paid a big price for breaking the rules.

God has been very clear in spelling out His moral expectations for man. He has also communicated the benefits and the penalties of keeping or violating His guidelines. Man is without excuse for knowing what God expects of him. In the Ten Commandments—the best-known statement on morals in history—God has revealed His moral standards.

## Morals from the Mountain

God summoned His chosen people, the nation of Israel, to come to the base of Mount Sinai. In that setting, God used Moses to conduct a massive orientation session on morality. God communicated His rules to the nation of Israel for governing their conduct. The account of that session is recorded in the book of Exodus.

1. Read Exodus 19. What indicates that God was serious about His rules?

That experience on Mount Sinai must have been a frightening event for the people of Israel. The exploding thunder, piercing lightning, rumbling earthquakes, and blasting trumpets would have left an unforgettable impression.

2. How might the boundaries, or fences, around the bottom of Mount Sinai represent God's moral limits?

In Exodus 20 God recorded the moral foundation of His law. The Ten Commandments comprise these rules. The study of the Commandments helps man to understand the moral guidelines by which God expects him to live.

3. How and when did you first hear of the Ten Commandments?

4. Where in society have these commandments been posted?

Many leaders in America's history believed these commandments provided essential moral guidelines. The nation's founding fathers considered God's laws an important entity in forming its social-moral structure. Sadly, in today's climate of political correctness and secularism, the influence of the Commandments' moral voice has been marginalized.

God intended that His people would use these commandments to guide their behavior. That meant that the people had to apply the commandments in their daily lives. The Ten Commandments affect a person's conduct.

### Commandment 1— "You shall have no other gods before Me" (Exodus 20:3).

Read Exodus 20:2 and 3.

God wasted no time when giving His commandments to establish His authority. He asserted that He set the standards for conduct. He began communicating His commandments by establishing His identity through His name, "I AM." When Moses was recording the events of Genesis, it was not the first time he had heard this name. While Moses was shepherding his sheep in a remote desert area, he came upon a physical phenomenon (Exodus 3:2, 3). A bush was burning but was not consumed by the fire. As Moses neared the bush, he realized that the bush was speaking. A voice from the bush was calling Moses by name, telling him not to approach. The bush ordered Moses to remove his shoes because he was standing on holy ground (vv. 4, 5). Moses immediately realized he was in the presence of God and hid his face in fear (v. 6).

As God spoke to Moses, He identified Himself by the name "I AM WHO I AM" (v. 14). This was the same name God used in Exodus 20:2. By this name God made it clear that He is completely self-sustaining. Unlike everyone and everything else in the universe that owes its existence to someone else, God derives His existence from no one but Himself. He is the Creator of all things and by Him all things exist (Colossians 1:16, 17). He didn't have a beginning point. No one created God! The bush that burned but was not consumed served as an object lesson of God's self-existence. Just as the fire did not depend on the bush as its fuel source, God did and does not depend on anything or anyone. As theologians say, *He is the uncaused cause.*

5. Why might have God used His "I AM WHO I AM" name as He began to give His ethical standards in Exodus 20:2 and 3?

When God stated, "You shall have no other gods before Me," He was making it clear that He expects complete and undivided allegiance.

6. How would your ethics be affected if you gave your allegiance to another final authority or divided your allegiance between authorities?

7. Who or what might vie for being the final authority of your life rather than the sovereign God?

8. How would your behavior be affected if these other authorities were setting the moral standards for your life instead of God?

9. (a)  How is the first commandment restated in Acts 14:15?

   (b)  Describe the verse's context (vv. 8–18).

10.  Do all religions have equal status in God's eyes according to the first commandment?

God began the statement of His ethical standards by demanding that He be the sole authority in all ethical decisions.

According to God, morality is to be His way or no way. Any moral guideline contrary to His standard is unacceptable.

Think about your life. How would you rank your adherence to God's standard as the final authority in all moral decisions you make? Indicate your response by marking an *X* on the line below.

**God's standard is my final authority when
making moral decisions.**

---

Never            Sometimes            Always

No human being has consistently lived up to God's standard of morality. Every person falls short. Man's shortcomings mean that he must face the consequences. Man's only hope is to seek mercy from the One Who sets the standards. The good news is that God wants to extend His mercy to all who call on His name.

## Commandment 2—
## "You shall not make for yourself a carved image" (Exodus 20:4).

Read Exodus 20:4.

In medieval times when a subject approached a king, the subject knelt before the ruler in a display of humble submission. Respectfully the subject might say to the king, "Lord, I am your loyal servant. Your wish is my command."

In the second commandment, God demanded that His subjects never carve nor form an image of anything before which they would bow and pledge their loyalty and service. God alone is the One Who deserves that homage. Despite the clarity of God's command, mankind has repeatedly violated this requirement.

11. What did God's people do at the base of Mount Sinai
    while God was giving His moral code to Moses (Exodus
    32:1–4)?




It had not been long since God had delivered the people
from the bondage of Egypt (Exodus 20:2). They had navigat-
ed through the Red Sea on dry ground by God's power (Exodus 14). They were even standing in the place at Mount Sinai
where they had witnessed the thunder, heard the trumpets,
and sworn they would do all that the Lord had spoken (Exodus 19:8).

12. Why do you think God's people were so quick to make
    a graven image?




13. What insight does Romans 1:18–25 provide into the
    rationale for man's fascination with images?




Man's intellectual arrogance causes him to remake a god
to fit his own ideas about deity. How convenient!

If I showed you a picture of my two children, you would
know something about them. If I made statues of them, you
might know a bit more. But you would never know everything
about them because you would only be looking at limited fac-
similes. To attempt to represent God by a man-made image,
you would reduce Him to nothing more than a limited facsim-
ile of your impressions. Keep in mind the name God used to

introduce Himself to Moses: "I AM WHO I AM." In this second commandment, it is as though He is saying, "Don't make me into something I AM not." Graven images do just that.

14. What does Psalm 115:3–8 say about the foolishness of trying to create an image of God?



Nothing compares to the true God. We must refuse any attempt to package Him in a form He is not.

15. What behaviors result from man's tailoring a god to suit his own preferences (Romans 1:22–32)?



The only accurate representation of God in human form is Jesus Christ.

16. What does Colossians 1:15–18 say about Jesus Christ?



17. How is the second commandment restated in 1 John 5:20 and 21?



You may not have religious statues or images in your possession, but you may have designed a god in your mind that is very different from the real God of the Bible. You may have formed a god who condones and even encourages conduct that would be unacceptable to the true God. I challenge you to take your god and place him next to God, Who has revealed Himself through His Word. If you are honest, you will discover that your god is a faux deity that can do nothing of eternal value for you. The true God is the only One before Whom you should bow in worship and service. He is the only One Who sets the final ethical standards.

### Commandment 3—
### "You shall not take the name of the LORD your God in vain" (Exodus 20:7).

Read Exodus 20:7.

My parents raised me to refer to older people using the terms "Mister," "Miss," or "Mrs." If a person had a title like "Doctor" or "Pastor," I was expected to use it when speaking to him. It was inappropriate for me to call my elders by their first names. The use of titles implied respect. If I were to refer to my elders by their first names, I would have categorized myself to be in their age bracket or station in life. Though I am older now, my throat still catches if I address esteemed men and women without their titles. I desire to show respect for their positions.

In the third commandment God demands that we do not take His name in vain (Exodus 20:7).

18.  How might a person violate the third commandment?


19.  (a)  What effect might taking the Lord's name in vain have on a person's behavior?


      (b)  Why do you think that might happen?

20. Name occasions when you have heard people taking the name of the Lord in vain.

21. Do you notice a correlation between this practice and a tolerance of lower moral standards in other areas of conduct?

22. How might the following activities of a Christian be adversely affected by taking the Lord's name in vain?
    (a) Praying (John 14:13, 14)

    (b) Singing (Colossians 3:16)

    (c) Speaking (Colossians 3:17)

    (d) Making promises (James 5:12)

Taking the Lord's name in vain is more than uttering a swearing expression. Just as with the previous commandments, this commandment requires having respect for authority. Does your behavior indicate that you have the utmost respect for God and that you will do whatever He commands?

23. How does behavior that disregards God's standards trivialize His name (Colossians 3:17)?

To disregard or disobey God's ethical standards is to suggest that God is not as important to you as He should be. In a sense you are taking the Lord's name in vain. When this commandment is viewed in this light, it follows that every person has violated its terms. Each individual is guilty and deserving of the consequences of his actions. He needs God's forgiveness.

Strive to maintain the utmost respect for God's name. Revere Him in a manner similar to the apostle Paul, who referred to Christ as being, "far above all principality and power and might and dominion, and every name that is named, not only in this age but also in that which is to come" (Ephesians 1:21).

# 5

# GOD'S WAY
# EVERY DAY

*For the believer, every day is sacred,
life is sacred, and parents are to be
honored.*

OFTEN people divide life into two categories—the sacred and the secular. Events of the workweek are viewed as secular, while times of worshiping and serving God and studying His Word are thought of as sacred. For the sake of consideration, assume that you view life in terms of these two categories. On the following chart, list your activities in a typical week for each of these categories.

| Sacred | Secular |
|--------|---------|
|        |         |
|        |         |
|        |         |
|        |         |

| Sacred | Secular |
|--------|---------|
|        |         |
|        |         |
|        |         |
|        |         |
|        |         |

If you were to take this divided approach to life, you would probably view God's demands on your behavior as being in the sacred category. With this approach, the activities under the secular category would not solely be under God's domain but would be open to ethical standards other than God's standards.

Think about the creation account in Genesis 1. In considering the seven days of the first week, which days were sacred and which were secular? In reality, God has His fingerprints on every portion of every day. He does not view the world He created as sacred and secular. The entire world is under His authority. Every hour of every day, 24/7, belongs in the sacred category. The Ten Commandments provide God's code of ethics for every part of your day—day after day.

### Commandment 4—
### "Remember the Sabbath day, to keep it holy" (Exodus 20:8).

Read Exodus 20:8–11.

1. What contrasting activities in a routine week are mentioned in Exodus 20:8–11?

Though the emphasis in this commandment appears to be the Sabbath, the passage actually refers to all seven days. The first six days are those in which God intended man to do his work. God set the precedent for this work schedule by accomplishing His creative labor in six days (Genesis 1).

In the fourth commandment, when God spoke of work, He was not simply referring to one's "job." God has used the term "work" to designate every responsibility that He has given to you. You may have a job, a family, and a home. You may be a student with study assignments. You may be involved in volunteer activities. You have service obligations at church. Whatever your responsibilities, God has called you to work and has prescribed the manner in which you are to do that work.

2. What does Ephesians 2:10 tell you about God's design for a believer?

3. Work is not a secular activity outside God's realm. God worked, and He assigned work to the first man. What moral guidelines has God established for your work?
   (a) Proverbs 6:6–11

   (b) Ephesians 6:5–9

    (c)  2 Thessalonians 3:7–15

    (d)  1 Peter 2:18–23

God has established ethical work standards. He expects you to do your work according to His code of conduct. Take stock of your work. If God conducted a year-end performance review with you, would He conclude that you never, sometimes, or always work according to His ethical standards?

**My work reflects God's ethical standards.**

---

Never                       Sometimes                   Always

## Time for a Break

In addition to work, God included a time to rest in the weekly schedule. You were not designed to work seven days a week. You need to break from the routine, sweat, toil, pressure, and demands of work to take time to relax, renew, and refocus your body, mind, and soul. In His law God designated a day to set work aside. He ordered His people to keep one day every week "holy" (Exodus 20:8). This day was to be set apart from the other six days and consecrated for a distinct purpose. Six days were for work; the seventh day was for rest from work.

4. Do you arrange your schedule to give yourself time to
rest? Describe your work and rest schedule.

God's people in the Old Testament were given specific
instructions in the law regarding religious practices to be followed on the Sabbath and other festival days.

5. According to Exodus 20:10, who was to rest?

6. What purpose and guidelines for the Sabbath do you
find in the following passages?
(a)  Exodus 31:12–17

(b)  Exodus 35:3

(c)  Exodus 16:4–36

(d)  Numbers 28:9, 10

(e)  Nehemiah 13:15–21

Those Jewish ceremonial days were instituted not merely
as ritual, but to foreshadow Christ. "So let no one judge you
in food or in drink, or regarding a festival or a new moon or

sabbaths, which are a shadow of things to come, but the substance is of Christ" (Colossians 2:16, 17; see also Hebrews 10:1).

When Christ came, the shadows were no longer necessary; He fulfilled all that previously had been only anticipated. New Testament believers no longer needed to practice the Sabbath as a day of ceremonial rest in anticipation of Christ.

Through faith in Christ's completed work on your behalf—His death, burial, and resurrection—you may enter into the privileges of rest in Him (Hebrews 4). He has taken away the record of your failed attempts to meet His demands. You can rest in the fact that you have been forgiven. "And you, being dead in your trespasses . . . He has made alive together with Him, having forgiven you all trespasses, having wiped out the handwriting of requirements that was against us, which was contrary to us. And He has taken it out of the way, having nailed it to the cross" (Colossians 2:13, 14). In His death Christ shed His blood to pay the penalty for your sinful shortcomings.

7. What offer did Christ extend (Matthew 11:28)?


8. What further explanation is provided in Ephesians 2:8 and 9?


The work of keeping God's moral requirements is beyond what any person can fulfill. The more a person labors to keep God's commandments, the more he recognizes he cannot meet the demands. Every person falls far short of God's ethical standards. However, all of God's demands are met in Jesus Christ. By placing your faith in Christ, you can cease from your labors and rest in Him.

The Old Testament people of God were to rest on the seventh day after six days of work. Now New Testament believers begin their week on the first day by remembering that they are resting in Christ's fulfillment of the demands of the law. Your worship on the first day of the week, Sunday, refreshes your soul as you feed on the Word and recall the work Christ accomplished. You can face the workweek ahead knowing that you do not have to work to achieve God's merit, but can rest in His approval because of Christ. Have you entered that rest, or are you still laboring to obtain God's approval? Come to Christ in faith and you will find rest.

## Commandment 5— "Honor your father and your mother" (Exodus 20:12).

Read Exodus 20:12.

The quote "A man's home is his castle" implies that in his castle, man is king. Inadvertently that idea may lead you to think that a man alone is the one who establishes the standards, or the rules, by which the household operates. In reality God's authority extends into the private world of your home life. God sets the rules for your home; He expects your family to follow His guidelines.

9. What do the following passages teach us about God's ethics for us at home?

    (a) Exodus 20:12


    (b) Proverbs 4:1–9

    (c)   Proverbs 31

    (d)   Colossians 3:18–21

10. Evaluate your home life. Do you recognize God as the final authority? Do all the members of your family live by His moral standards? Rank your family's behavior.

**Our family lives by God's guidelines.**

| Never | Sometimes | Always |
|---|---|---|

Homes that operate by God's standard are not free of problems, yet they can be lighthouses that radiate God's glory to the surrounding neighborhood. Matthew 5:14–16 says, "You are the light of the world. A city that is set on a hill cannot be hidden. Nor do they light a lamp and put it under a basket, but on a lampstand, and it gives light to all who are in the house. Let your light so shine before men, that they may see your good works and glorify your Father in heaven."

The mission of being God's lighthouse became evident to my wife and me many years ago. A neighbor lady, the wife of an abusive husband, knocked on our back door and asked if she might speak with us. She tearfully said, "I look out the back window of my home and see you and your family. I think to myself, That's what my family should be like." We had a wonderful opportunity to emphasize that we were not a perfect family, but that our faith in Christ allowed God to work through us. That visit was a sobering reminder that we are to live before others so that God may be glorified.

## Commandment 6—
## "You shall not murder" (Exodus 20:13).

Read Exodus 20:13.

Every January many churches recognize "Sanctity of Human Life Day." It is an occasion to remind people of the value of human life and to decry the sinful acts of abortion and euthanasia. In God's view, every day is sanctity-of-life day. When God gave His Ten Commandments, He stated in unequivocal terms that murder is unacceptable (Exodus 20:13).

11. What forms of murder take place in today's world?

12. According to Genesis 1:26 and 27, why is man's life so valuable?

No animal or plant bears the image of God. Only man wears this badge of distinction. God expects mankind to recognize that every person is made in His image. That image may be buried under crusty layers of sin, but it is still there nonetheless.

You might tend to dismiss this commandment personally. It appears to be an easy command for you to keep; you do not view yourself as a murderer. Before you quickly pat yourself on the back, pause to consider what the Bible says regarding this commandment.

13. Why do you think 1 John 3:15 equates hatred with murder?

14. What forms of hatred might Christians be guilty of committing?

15. What high moral standards did Christ introduce in Matthew 5:38–48?

16. What new commandment did Christ give in John 13:34 and 35?

Instead of hatred, violence, and murder, God desires that you demonstrate self-control, respect, and compassion toward your fellow man and even toward those who wrong you.

17. Examine your conduct and conversations over the last month. Would you say you have consistently followed the example of Christ? Do you see any traces of murder in your behavior or words? Remember to evaluate yourself by the standard of Christ. How do you measure up? Rank yourself.

**I live by God's perfect standard of love.**

---

Never                        Sometimes                        Always

You may be feeling overwhelmed by the ethical demands of the Ten Commandments. When you honestly consider the moral implications of God's law and then assess your obedience, you will admit that you can't meet the standards 100 percent of the time.

If the saying "Misery loves company" is true, you can be assured that you have plenty of company. As Romans 3:23 says, "For all have sinned and fall short of the glory of God."

If you are sensing your guilt after considering the first five commandments, take a deep breath, because five more commandments remain. Remember these words of hope in Romans 5:6–8: "For when we were still without strength, in due time Christ died for the ungodly. For scarcely for a righteous man will one die; yet perhaps for a good man someone would even dare to die. But God demonstrates His own love toward us, in that while we were still sinners, Christ died for us." Christ provides forgiveness from your moral shortcomings.

# 6

# THE PERFECT TEN

*God expects us not only to respect*
*others but also to protect them by what*
*we do not do.*

ONE OF THE gravest mistakes we can make is to deceive ourselves into thinking that we are morally invincible. In his book *A Code of Jewish Ethics,* Joseph Telushkin tells a story that stresses the importance of honesty in ethical self-awareness.

> The nineteenth-century Chasidic rebbe Chayim of Sanz asked a man what he would do if he found a wallet with a great deal of money inside it. "I'd return it to the owner immediately," the man said.
>
> "Are you really so sure?" the rebbe challenged him.
>
> When he posed the same question to a second person, the man responded, "I'd keep it. When else will I have an opportunity to get money so easily?"
>
> The rebbe told the man that such behavior was reprehensible.
>
> When he asked the question of a third man, the man responded, "How can I be certain what I'd

do? I know that I must return it, but how can I be
sure that I would? I pray to God that I would have
the strength to overcome my evil inclination and
return it."

It was only this last response, combining both the
man's awareness of his potential for dishonesty
and his desire to do good, that pleased the rebbe.
(Joseph Telushkin, *The Code of Jewish Ethics*, vol. 1,
*You Shall Be Holy* [New York: Harmony/Bell Tower,
2006].)

Mark 10:17–22 is the account of a man well-versed in
Jewish ethics who approached Jesus. Confidently he boasted
that he had kept all of the commandments from his youth.
Compassionately Jesus confronted the man's presumption by
suggesting that he do a morally magnanimous deed and sell
all his possessions, give the money to the poor, and then take
up the life of Christ as a follower. The man went away sorrow-
ful because he had great possessions with which he would not
part. The reality of his flawed moral condition was uncovered
by a revealing confrontation with God's standards. He refused
to honestly and humbly admit his shortcomings and submit to
God's demands. He was not as ethically invincible as he had
led others and himself to believe.

Studying God's moral standards is never an easy task because you will inevitably come face-to-face with your flawed
moral character. Yet that realization is not a bad thing. For it
is by realizing your sinful condition that you will be ready to
seek mercy from God.

1. What did Paul say is the value of God's law (Romans
   7:7–12)?

As you study the remaining Commandments, ask God to use His Word to reveal areas of your moral shortcomings. The starting point for change is your awareness of your moral condition.

## Commandment 7—
## "You shall not commit adultery" (Exodus 20:14).

Read Exodus 20:14.

Anyone who is familiar with human resources policies of a for-profit business knows that every employee is entitled to certain rights of privacy. For instance, an employer may not ask on an application about race, age, health conditions (unless warranted by job requirements), marital status, sexual orientation, or religion. Those factors are viewed as matters that should have no bearing on a person's ability to perform a job. An employer does not have permission to probe into certain personal areas.

It is common to think that a person's private life is not subject to moral inspection. An ad campaign for the city of Las Vegas stated, "What happens in Vegas, stays in Vegas." The slogan suggested that when a person visits Las Vegas, he or she is no longer accountable for behavior to people back home.

God operates by a different set of ethical parameters. His standards extend into every area of your life. They apply not only in public, but behind the closed doors of bedrooms, in parked cars, behind the passwords of computers, and even in the seclusion of your thoughts.

2. How is the seventh commandment restated in the New Testament (1 Corinthians 6:9, 10)?

3. What moral standards regarding sexuality has God established in the following passages?

(a)  Exodus 20:14

(b)  Matthew 5:27, 28

(c)  1 Corinthians 6:12–20

(d)  1 Corinthians 7:1–5

(e)  1 Thessalonians 4:1–8

Human sexuality is a gift from God that is to be enjoyed in a loving, respectful manner only within the prescribed relationship of marriage between a man and a woman. Every man must consider carefully the implications of godly ethical standards in the relevant area of sexual conduct.

## Commandment 8—
## "You shall not steal" (Exodus 20:15).

Read Exodus 20:15.

Anybody who likes adventure stories often finds narratives of robberies fascinating. The scheming and execution involved in pulling off a heist make for intriguing, edge-of-your-seat drama.

4. Describe an account of a robbery that has captured your interest.


Chances are you would never consider planning and executing a robbery. For this reason you might dismiss the eighth commandment before even considering it. However, this law has implications for you.

5. Write a brief summary of the moral precept in each of the following passages.
   (a)  Exodus 22:1–15


   (b)  Leviticus 19:13–15


   (c)  Leviticus 19:35, 36


   (d)  Leviticus 25:35–38


6. How is the eighth commandment restated in the New Testament (Ephesians 4:28)?


7. Based upon the preceding moral precepts from the law, how might the following individuals be tempted to steal?

(a)  Lumber salesman

(b)  Employer of migrant workers

(c)  Oil company executive

(d)  Farmer

(e)  Government contractor

8. How would violating another person's right of ownership have a damaging effect on society?

God does not want you to take from someone else that which does not belong to you. Your business dealings matter to God. His ethics extend into your finances, your job, and the marketplace.

### Commandment 9—
### "You shall not bear false witness against your neighbor" (Exodus 20:16).

Read Exodus 20:16.

A coach for a major university was dismissed from his position for falsifying information on his résumé. A lie cost him

his job. A high school student was humiliated among her class-
mates and teachers because another student shared false stories about her. A lie destroyed friendships and left emotional
scars on a fragile adolescent. The handling of information
matters to God.

9. Using the first person pronoun *I*, write the ninth com-
    mandment (Exodus 20:16) in your own words.

10. How is this moral guideline restated in the New Testa-
    ment (Colossians 3:9, 10)?

11. Describe the serious consequences that might occur if
    misinformation was used in the following settings:
    (a)  Courtroom

    (b)  Job application

    (c)  Military intelligence

    (d)  Newsroom

    (e)  Historical accounts

In the realm of communication, truth is an endangered species. God, Who identifies Himself as truth (John 14:6) and Whose nature has never or will never permit Him to lie (Titus 1:2), demands that you always communicate truthfully. Take a moment to assess your communication. How would you rank yourself on the following scale?

**I communicate truthfully.**

| Never | Sometimes | Always |
|---|---|---|

## Commandment 10— "You shall not covet" (Exodus 20:17).

Read Exodus 20:17.

In 1994 the world of championship figure skating witnessed a bizarre, blatant occurrence of unsportsmanlike conduct. Two rivals, Tonya Harding and Nancy Kerrigan, were vying for the coveted title of American figure skating champion. As the competition unfolded, it became apparent that Nancy Kerrigan was the better skater. Tonya Harding desired the title to such an extent that she became involved in a plot in which two men were hired to attack Nancy Kerrigan. The men repeatedly hit Kerrigan on her leg with a baton, causing a serious injury that required the talented skater to withdraw from the competition. In the absence of Kerrigan, Tonya Harding was awarded the title. A short time later the plot was uncovered; Tonya Harding was stripped of her title, fined $100,000, and banned for life from the U.S. Figure Skating Association.

A controlling desire had been festering inside Tonya Harding to have what belonged to her opponent. This desire is the focus of the tenth commandment (Exodus 20:17)—the act of coveting. Closely related to coveting are the acts of envying and being jealous.

In the normal course of events, you will see things that you would like to possess. Who hasn't window-shopped online or in a store? This type of daydreaming can be a harmless activity until the desire takes an evil turn. The person's deeds turn to looking on another's belongings, wanting the other's possessions, and scheming to get the objects of desire.

12. How do the following accounts illustrate the evil potential inherent in coveting?

    (a)  Laban toward Jacob (Genesis 31)

    (b)  Jacob's sons toward their brother Joseph (Genesis 37)

    (c)  Saul toward David (1 Samuel 18:5–12)

    (d)  David toward Bathsheba (2 Samuel 11)

    (e)  Ahab toward Naboth (1 Kings 21:1–26)

In each of these situations, coveting fostered a series of violations of God's moral standards and resulted in complications. The consequences for these violations were serious.

13. How is the tenth commandment restated in the New Testament (Ephesians 5:3)?

14. What might cause a man to not observe this command?

15. How can a man violate this command without anyone knowing what he is doing?

16. How would the sin of coveting eventually surface in actions?

## The Big Picture

Taken together, these commandments form the skeleton of God's ethical standards. God wants you to think carefully about everything you do, say, and think. He demands that you live His way.

When you assess your life in light of the demands of the entire law, how do you fare? You may compare yourself to someone else and think, "At least I'm not that bad."

17. What do you learn in James 2:8–11 that foils any attempt at self-justification?

18. What do Romans 3:19 and 20 tell you about your stand-
    ing according to the standard of the law?


   As Romans 3:23 explains, every person has sinned and
come short of the perfect ethical standard God has established. You cannot meet God's moral demands. You will always come up short, no matter how hard you try or how good
you think you may be. There is nothing you can do in yourself
to help your situation. Your only hope is to discover the great
truth of God's love and grace that can forgive your sin and
reconcile your relationship with the God Whose standards
you violated.
   Read Romans 5:6–21 and answer the following questions.

19. What did Christ do for you when you were without moral
    strength (v. 6)?


20. How did Christ demonstrate His love for you (v. 8)?


21. What does Christ's blood achieve for you if you believe
    in Him (v. 9)?


22. What is a believer's relationship with God through
    Christ's death and life (vv. 10, 11)?

23. What was the consequence for sin that started with Adam and was passed to all men (vv. 12–14)?

24. What was Christ able to accomplish through His death for the many who believe in Him (vv. 15–19)?

25. What exceeds the sin that the law reveals (vv. 20, 21)?

God's law reveals your sin, but God's grace will forgive your sin and give you the confident assurance that you are reconciled with God and have eternal life. Through Christ's death you can be saved from the consequences of your sin (Romans 6:23).

26. Read Romans 10:9–13. What response does this passage call you to make in order to be saved?

27. Have you made that response? If not, do so now and you will be saved. Pray this prayer to God: Lord, I know that I am a sinner; I have violated your moral standards. I am worthy of death for my sin. But now I believe in Christ, Whose death and resurrection paid the penalty for my sin. Thank You for saving me.

# 7

# More than
# the Don'ts

*The "nots" of God's Word are intended
for our well-being.*

A T TIMES nonbelievers stereotype Christianity as a negative religion composed primarily of "thou shalt not" rules. Their association of Christianity with a "don't-do" list gives them fodder for belittling and rejecting the faith.

Even believers may accumulate negative perceptions of Christianity. Possibly they grew up in a home where a parent was highly critical of their behavior. They may never have been able to please their dads or their moms. Whatever they did was never quite good enough. All they heard was "don't do this" or "don't do that." From their experiences they associate Christianity with "do not" imperatives.

Other believers may view the church as having a negative atmosphere, characterized by legalism and oppression. They believe church members are waiting and watching for them to step out of line. They fear being reprimanded from the pulpit for violating the rules.

A careful study of the Bible does reveal "thou shalt nots," because God clearly forbids certain conduct as unacceptable.

1. How many of the Ten Commandments are stated in the negative (Exodus 20:1–17)?

2. What are some other examples of ethical guidelines stated in the negative in Scripture?

The teachers of the Old Testament law identified 613 commandments that God communicated in the Torah, the first five books of the Bible. Legal scholars categorized 365 of those commandments as negative, and 248 as positive.

While the Bible contains "do nots," it also contains "dos." A believer is not only to avoid certain actions, but also to carry out positive actions. For every restriction in the Bible, there is a counterbalancing positive action. When God demands that we not lie, He also demands that we speak truthfully. God requires that we not steal but also asks us to share generously.

3. For each "don't" to heed, write a "do" to fulfill when responding to God's ethical standards.

| Responding to God's Ethical Standards | |
|---|---|
| *Don't* | *Do* |
| Make idols | |
| Covet | |
| Commit adultery | |

| Responding to God's Ethical Standards | |
|---|---|
| *Don't* | *Do* |
| Gossip | |
| Hate | |
| Be slothful | |
| Pervert justice | |
| Hold a grudge | |
| Seek revenge | |

4. When you respond to God's ethical standards, are you known for what you don't do more than for what you do?

5. How did Jesus summarize the entire law in two positive commandments (Mark 12:28–31)?

Consider examples of the positive side of morality. For instance, a husband may never have been unfaithful to his wife, but has he shown her kindness, respect, tenderness, and love? The Bible requires not only that he avoid the negative action of marital unfaithfulness, but also that he demonstrate the positive action of godly conduct.

6. What positive conduct is a husband to demonstrate toward his wife (Ephesians 5:25–30; 1 Peter 3:7–9)?

How would you rank yourself in obedience to the Biblical command of loving and respecting your wife?

**I treat my wife with love and respect as the Bible instructs.**

| | | |
|---|---|---|
| Never | Sometimes | Always |

A father has not fulfilled his moral obligations toward his children simply because he has procreated and does not abuse his offspring. God also expects a father to fulfill his ethical responsibility to influence his children with Biblical instruction.

7. What positive moral duties does a father have toward his children (Ephesians 6:1–4; Deuteronomy 6:6–9)?

8. What illustration of fatherly instruction for a son is given in Proverbs 5?

God requires that fathers actively teach their children Biblical principles for wise living. A father who does not warn his son or daughter about the dangers of getting involved romantically with the wrong person would be morally negligent. Failing to teach wisdom principles is like leaving a child unprotected from a vicious animal. If a dangerous dog were in the neighborhood, a good father would make every effort to guard his child against an attack. Sexual predators are as dangerous as rabid animals. Fathers have a serious moral obligation to teach their children God's wisdom for proper relationships.

If you are a father, how would you rank your obedience to teaching your children wisdom principles from the Word of God?

### I consistently teach my children wisdom principles from God's Word.

| Never | Sometimes | Always |
|-------|-----------|--------|

If a son has displayed compliance and respect toward his mother in public yet neglects her in her later years, he has fallen short of his ethical duties. The Bible requires that a son and his family demonstrate special care toward his mother when she becomes a widow.

9. What responsibility does a son and his family have toward his widowed mother (1 Timothy 5:3, 4)?

10. How did God view neglect of a widow by her family (1 Timothy 5:7, 8)?

God placed a high priority on the compassionate care of society's most vulnerable members. Widows and orphans often had no means of protection or provision. God considered the care of these needy people to be among the most poignant demonstrations of genuine faith. According to James 1:27, acts of sacrificial love toward orphans and widows are a sign of authentic Christianity. Conversely, God displayed righteous indignation when these helpless individuals were neglected. Despite specific instruction from God about the ethical obligation a family has toward an elderly widowed mother, God's people in the Old Testament repeatedly neglected this most humble act of service.

11. What responsibility does a church have toward a widow who has no means of support from her family (1 Timothy 5:3–10)?

How would you rank your obedience to this ethical obligation to care for widows?

**I show compassionate care toward widows in my family and church.**

| Never | Sometimes | Always |
|---|---|---|

God requires that you not covet your neighbors' possessions. However, God extends your responsibility toward your neighbors beyond that prohibition. He asks that you carry out compassionate acts toward your neighbors. The gospel of Luke records the account of a man who was a serious student of the Old Testament law. Seeking to justify himself, he wanted to demonstrate to Jesus his loyalty to the law. In light of the command to love one's neighbor as oneself, the man asked, "Who is my neighbor?"

12. What answer to the man's question did Jesus give in the parable of the Good Samaritan (Luke 10:25–37)?

13. What acts of compassion did the Samaritan man extend to the injured victim (Luke 10:34, 35)?

14. Name situations in which God would want you to lend assistance toward a person in need.


Rank your response to the command of loving your neighbor as yourself.

**I demonstrate compassion toward my neighbor.**

| | | |
|---|---|---|
| Never | Sometimes | Always |

Think how different the world would be if everyone lived by the ethical standard of the Golden Rule. That ideal cannot be realized in a sin-cursed world. However, as an individual, you can make a difference! Determine that by God's help you will show compassion toward your neighbor.

15. God's ethical standards extend into every dimension of your life, including the workplace. What ethical standards does God expect to be in place on your job?


16. In your list of workplace ethics, did you include the duties found in the following passages? Identify the ethical requirement in each passage.
    (a)  1 Timothy 6:1, 2


    (b)  Colossians 4:1


    (c)  1 Peter 2:18–23

18. How would you rate yourself in terms of carrying out God's ethical standards on the job?

**I do my job by God's ethical standards.**

| | | |
|---|---|---|
| Never | Sometimes | Always |

Many businesses are recognizing the importance of workplace ethics. They commit time, money, and training to raise their employees' standard of ethical conduct on the job.

19. From the news media or personal experience, describe negative business situations that could have had different outcomes if people had followed proper ethical practices.

Prejudice, racial slurs, and ethnic hostilities have no place in the life of a believer. Yet sometimes Christians are careless with their words and actions in this sensitive area.

20. What lessons do you infer or learn from the following passages regarding the way you should view and treat people?
    (a) James 2:1–13

    (b) Revelation 5:8, 9

    (c) Genesis 5:1, 2

21. How would you rank yourself regarding your attitude toward people who are racially or economically different from you?

**I treat people with dignity, regardless of their race or station in life.**

| | | |
|---|---|---|
| Never | Sometimes | Always |

In the course of your life, you have most likely been wronged by another person. Someone did something hurtful or unjust to you. Unfair treatment is a reality of life. What is man's natural response when someone has wronged him? Most likely when someone is unfairly wronged, he will choose the path of retaliation.

22. What additional standards of conduct does the Bible communicate in the following passages?
    (a)  Matthew 5:43–48

    (b)  Matthew 18:15–17

    (c)  Matthew 18:21–35

    (d)  Romans 12:17–21

As you can see from these standards of Biblical ethics, God places significant demands on your conduct. God's standards are as high as His own flawless character and perfect actions. All of this may seem overwhelming because these requirements appear to be greater than what you are able to perform.

23. What honest self-assessment did Paul provide regarding his efforts to consistently demonstrate ethical conduct (Romans 7:14–25)?

Even when you become a follower of Christ, you have a constant challenge to live in a holy manner. You cannot do it on your own. Thankfully God is well aware of your weakness. His grace is available to enable you to live in a manner consistent with His standards.

24. What wonderful assistance is available to a believer in managing his conduct (2 Peter 1:2–4)?

When you know and rely on Jesus Christ and the grace He makes available to those who trust in Him, you will discover the assistance to live the ethically holy life God called you to live.

Take a few moments to ponder your conduct. Ask God to show you areas of your behavior that need improvement (Psalm 139:23, 24). Now ask God to help you begin a serious study of Biblical ethics that will result in behavioral transformation in which you will become increasingly like Christ.

# 8

# YOU DECIDE

*The choice to be ethical is part of our*
*everyday experiences.*

WHEN you hear the word "ethics," you might picture a philosopher, far removed from the normal world, thoughtfully pondering the implications of mankind's actions. You may have heard the term "ethics" being used in discussions related to lifestyle choices, euthanasia, abortion, weapons of mass destruction, or stem cell research. While these subjects are important, they represent a small fraction of the myriad of ethical issues that you face in everyday life. Daily you are confronted with a multitude of ethical issues to which you must actively respond. Hopefully your response will reflect your faith in Jesus Christ and your willingness to follow His instruction.

Having a head full of Bible knowledge does not automatically guarantee that you will respond wisely to life's situations. Though you may be able to win the Bible category of the Jeopardy game show, God desires that your faith makes a much greater impact in your life. God's Word is meant to become embedded in your being so that you are transformed in your thinking, character, conversations, and behavior to progressively be more like Christ.

Your faith is to be more than performing outward rituals, such as attending church or performing acts of Christian service. Repeatedly in the Old Testament God confronted His people with the stark reality that they were acknowledging Him outwardly but were wandering far from Him inwardly. His intent in calling them for His own was that their changed hearts would yield right behavior. Their conduct was to be a vivid testimony before the pagan world of His holiness and grace.

Micah 6:6 and 7 ask a series of pointed questions to emphasize that God is not satisfied with mere religious ritual. Ironically He is not satisfied even with the ritual He initiated in His law. "With what shall I come before the LORD, And bow myself before the High God? Shall I come before Him with burnt offerings, With calves a year old? Will the LORD be pleased with thousands of rams, Ten thousand rivers of oil? Shall I give my firstborn for my transgression, The fruit of my body for the sin of my soul?"

Instead of religious ritual, God states clearly that His greatest desire is for your life to be characterized by godly conduct consistent with His holiness. "He has shown you, O man, what is good; And what does the LORD require of you But to do justly, To love mercy, And to walk humbly with your God?" (Micah 6:8). All of these behavioral expectations are ethical in nature.

This final lesson challenges you to exercise your ethical decision-making skills. Remember, a Biblical approach to ethics always begins with God. How would God want you to respond to these ethical situations?

## What a Deal?

A college student sits on his bed, looking at the tuition bill he just received from the registrar's office. The cost is staggering. To make matters worse, he has just received the required book lists from his instructors. He calculates the cost of the textbooks will bury him financially. One class alone requires him to purchase computer software, costing nearly $1,000. A friend who is taking the same class knows of this student's tight finances. He has purchased the same software and offers it to this student to download free of charge.

1. In light of this generous offer, should the student dismiss the reality of copyright infringement and download his friend's software?

2. Should the enormous profitability of the software company have any bearing on the student's decision?

3. What is the Biblical basis for your response?

4. What moral obligation does the student have toward his friend?

## Cashing in by the Pound

A father recognizes that his son has exceptional athletic ability. His son's coach has indicated that the young man has the potential for obtaining a full scholarship to a major university. Candidly the coach explains that the competition for these schools is fierce. The father realizes that he could significantly increase the chances of his son's landing the scholarship if his son could bulk up his weight and muscle mass. The father knows that certain dietary supplements and injections could help his son make the jump to the next level of physical development. The father is aware that these products are on the banned list. The student has told his father that many of his teammates are gaining a physical advantage by taking these supplements and that the school has not implemented a drug testing policy.

5. Should the father encourage his son to take the supplements? Why or why not?

6. How might the father explain his decision to his son?

7. What is the Biblical basis for your response?

8. Do the father and son have any moral obligation toward the coach and other members of the team? Why or why not?

## Office Confidential

An executive assistant with a publicly traded company has been accumulating company stock since he began working with the firm many years ago. Upon hearing a confidential discussion among company administrators, the executive assistant becomes aware of an impending lawsuit against the company regarding one of its products. Most likely the public announcement will affect the value of the company stock. The executive assistant has an opportunity to sell some of his company stock before its value declines. He assumes that his role within the company will not make him a suspect for insider trading violations. In addition, he has promised to use a portion of the stock proceeds to assist a worthy ministry.

9. What should the executive assistant do with his stock?

10. Does the executive assistant have a responsibility to consider how his decision affects the stockholders (his co-workers) who are unaware of this confidential information?

11. Does the executive assistant have an obligation to the ministry organization he promised to help? Why or why not?

12. What is the Biblical basis for your response?

## Guess Who's Living Next Door

The community in which you have lived for many years is ethnically homogeneous. The vast majority of the residents are descendants from a specific region of Europe. The community is abuzz with news that a house for sale has been purchased by a family from a country far removed from the town's ethnic roots. The townspeople view themselves as having a superior lineage and begin making comments about declining property values. Residents suggest that more families of this nationality may begin moving into the neighborhood. Some community members infer that this influx will bring danger to children and pose a threat to the quality of education in the school district.

13. How do you respond?


14. What moral obligation do you have to the new family?


15. Do you have any moral obligation to your long-term community friends and neighbors? Why or why not?


16. What is the Biblical basis for your response?

17. What steps should you take to respond to this situation?

## A Warm Greeting

The relationship between a man and his wife has cooled. His wife has been experiencing chronic health problems for an extended time. A new family has moved in next door. The man sees the husband and wife doing yard work, and he goes over to welcome them into the neighborhood. The neighbor's wife is very outgoing. In future encounters she always goes out of her way to greet the man in a warm, friendly manner. It is not long before this man finds himself thinking about and watching for the woman next door. He begins comparing her to his wife.

18. What ethical issues apply to this scenario?

19. What should this man do?

20. What is the Biblical basis for your response?

21. What would be the effects of an improper ethical decision?

## Annoying Procedures

A manager in a retail store is responsible to inventory all incoming deliveries to ensure the arrival of all the ordered products. Company policy requires him to complete the paperwork at the time of the delivery—initialing every item on the invoice as it is received, signing the receipt for the delivery person, and dating the form that will be reviewed by the company auditor. On a recent delivery day when the manager's schedule was quite hectic, he instructed the delivery person to unload the items, but he did not take the time to inventory each item in the delivery. He signed the receipt for the delivery person, acknowledging that the order was complete in its delivery. He relied on the fact that the delivery company has had a good track record with its deliveries. Two days later he learns that his company's auditor will be visiting the store. He quickly inventories the sent items and considers the idea of backdating the form to meet the auditing requirements.

22. Would it be acceptable for the manager to backdate the form since all the products were received? Why or why not?


23. What should the manager say to the auditor?


24. What is the Biblical basis for your response?

## That Hurts

As you work on a home remodeling project, you injure yourself. You recognize that the injury could keep you from work for a period of time, but the fact that the injury occurred at home means you will not be covered by workmen's compensation. Your finances are very tight, so you do not have the option of taking time off from work. You struggle into work the next day and experience an additional minor injury. You notify your supervisor, and he assumes that all of your injuries occurred on the job. His assumption would make it possible for you to apply for workmen's compensation and obtain an income stream while recuperating at home.

25. Is it appropriate to submit the claim under these circumstances? Why or why not?

26. Do you have any moral obligation to your supervisor and to your company? Why or why not?

27. What is the Biblical basis for your response?

## On the Road to the Nobel Prize

Your daughter is preparing a science project for the annual school science fair. The science fair guidelines permit you to work with your daughter on determining the idea for the project but require that she do the actual project research and preparation. You are aware that in previous years students received substantial assistance from their parents in putting their projects together. This parental participation enabled the students to get high grades on their science fair projects. You realize that if you stick by the guidelines and entrust the work to your child, she will probably receive a lesser grade than the children who receive parental assistance.

28. Do you follow the science fair guidelines? Why or why not?

29. What is the Biblical basis for your conclusion?

30. How should you communicate your conclusion to your daughter?

31. Do you have any moral obligation toward the teacher and the other students and parents?

### Another Motel Room

Your job with a large corporation requires you to be away from home two days a week. You often lodge in hotels which are part of a chain that has a corporate account with your company. As a perk to recruit and keep the corporation's business, the hotel offers your company's employees access to free in-room movies, including pornographic films. The hotel does not reference specific movie titles on their billing. The prospect of watching these late-night films seems appealing, as your physical relationship with your wife is not good.

32. What is your response in this situation?

33. What is the Biblical basis for your response?

34. What steps will you take to deal with this situation?

## The High Cost of Suspicion

A student in the junior Sunday School class that you teach has been acting strangely in recent weeks. You have observed that she has become increasingly detached and angry. You suspect that something unsettling is going on in her life. You question her and sense that she is resisting telling you the truth about her circumstances and that she is fearful. On Sunday afternoon you receive a phone call from the child's father. He is upset because his daughter was crying after Sunday School. He wants to know what you said to his daughter. He angrily insists that you have no right to have personal conversations with her. The father is an important businessman in town and an influential church member. The call and your observations over the next month lead you to believe that something inappropriate is happening in that family.

35. What do you do?

36. What is your moral obligation to the child?

37. What is your moral obligation to the parents?

38. What is your moral obligation to the church?

39. What is the Biblical basis for your response?

Everything you do has ethical implications. Some situations you face will be complex, requiring thoughtful deliberation. Most instances are simple, everyday occurrences that require immediate responses. All demand that you act in a manner consistent with God's ethics. The ethical goal toward which God wants you to live is summed up in this challenge: "Therefore, whether you eat or drink, or whatever you do, do all to the glory of God" (1 Corinthians 10:31).

# WRAP IT UP

TODAY, tomorrow, and every day for the rest of your life, God has called you as a man to be holy like He is holy. It would be nice if it were as easy to live a holy life as it is to talk about it. But living in a holy manner is easier said than done. Holiness requires you to diligently study God's behavioral standards as revealed in His Word so you can determine right conduct. Holiness also calls for you to resist daily forces that would pull you to live by a set of behavioral standards that are unholy or contrary to God's Word. Determine by God's grace to behave God's way. If you do, here is what Christ said you can expect: "If you keep My commandments, you will abide in My love, just as I have kept My Father's commandments and abide in His love. These things I have spoken to you, that My joy may remain in you, and that your joy may be full" (John 15:10, 11). Discover the joy of living God's way!

# ANSWERS

**Lesson 1**

1.

| Setting | Rules | Consequence of Ignoring Rules |
|---------|-------|-------------------------------|
| Sports | Baseball—Balk<br>Golf—Ball repositioning | Batter takes base<br>Penalty stroke |
| Community | Speed limit<br>Parking | Ticket<br>Ticket |
| School | Time for start of class<br>No talking during test | Demerits or detention<br>Demerits or detention |
| Workplace | Treatment of opposite sex<br><br>Accurate reporting of income to IRS | Warning, possible job termination, lawsuit<br>Fine |

2. Every man did what was right in his own eyes.

3. Answers may vary. Activities such as meal preparation, driving, doing your job, dealing with neighbors over property lines, paying for products in stores, and dealing with family relationships.

4. Parents, teachers, pastors, civic officials, coaches, military officers, God.

5. Division of day and night, of atmosphere, of water and land; plants and animals reproduce after their kind; stellar bodies in place.

6. Position of authority over animals; made in image of God; reproduction between man and woman; use of plants for food.

7. God. He is the creator.

8. No rain, but a mist provided to water the ground.

9. Adam was to tend the Garden; he was permitted to eat of every tree but one; he could find no compatible partner among the animals; he was to be joined to a wife.

10. God. He created all things.

11. Personal answers.

12. The man would not perceive an obligation to accept God's ethical standards.

13. They did not glorify Him as God. They perceived Him to be on the same level as created beings.

14. Man appointed himself as the authority.

15. Unfitting activities (from God's perspective), such as sexual immortality, covetousness, murder, and backbiting.

16. Answers may vary; for example, behavioral standards such as homosexuality did not follow God's design of a man with a woman.

17. Cause a corrupt and chaotic society with little respect for people; a flourishing of debased moral practices.

18. Men disregard the threat of God's judgment and approve those who refuse His standard.

19. Answers will vary.

## Lesson 2

1. Serpent (Satan), woman (Eve), man (Adam).
2. God.
3. God.
4. Duties—Dominion over living animals; multiply; subdue the earth; eat from herbs and trees; tend the Garden. Moral boundary—Do not eat of the tree of knowledge of good and evil.
5. To disregard the moral boundary and eat from the tree.
6. They ate the fruit of the tree.
7. You will die.
8. Shame, embarrassment, concealment.
9. Fear, shame, guilt.
10. Blame others.
11. (a) Serpent—Cursed more than other animals; move on belly; eat dust; experience enmity with "the woman;" suffer a bruised head. (b) Eve—Sorrow and pain in childbearing; desire for husband; ruled over by husband. (c) Adam—Ground is cursed; hard work; return to dust. (d) Mankind—Sin passed on all men; death.
12. Knowledge of good and evil.
13. The capacity exists to know, create, and do evil. Mankind is inherently evil.
14. Anger.
15. Toward Abel and ultimately toward God. It expressed rebellion toward God's authority.
16. Personal answers.
17. Because it was sin.
18. Personal answers.
19. You can do what is right, or you can give in to the sinful desire.
20. Killed him.
21. He gave an excuse, refusing to accept responsibility for his brother's welfare. He was dishonest and lacked compassion.
22. Unproductive ground; a fugitive; a marked man; out of God's presence.
23. God said that every intent and thought of man was continually evil.
24. (a) Noah—just; perfect; walked with God. (b) Humanity—corrupt; violent.
25. He determined to destroy man.
26. Worldwide flood and destruction.

27. God viewed Noah with grace and enjoyed fellowship with him. Noah and his family were spared from destruction.

28. Personal answers.

## Lesson 3

1. His inherent evil.

2. Multiply; fill the earth; recognize that all things are given to man; do not eat flesh with blood in it; do not murder another person.

3. (a) Family—What are God's standards for family planning regarding marriage and children? (b) Animals—Does this passage suggest that it is permissible for man to hunt and fish? (c) Diet—Does God impose any dietary restrictions on man? (d) Dignity of human life—What is God's view of capital punishment?

4. (a) Family—Man disparages marriage and accepts same-sex unions. (b) Animals—Man exalts animals and worships them. (c) Diet—Man abstains from certain foods for "religious" reasons. (d) Dignity of human life—Man murders and has disputes.

5. He fell asleep naked in his tent.

6. To not think clearly; to become unrestrained.

7. A curse was pronounced on Ham's son because Ham violated God's standards. Blessing came to Shem and Japheth for obeying God's standards.

8. His actions affect the family, resulting in sin, pain, division, and conflict.

9. Stay away from alcoholic beverages; they are dangerous.

10. Personal answers.

11. You should think of the other people in your life and about how your course of action will affect them.

12. A tall tower, reaching into the heavens.

13. To make a statement of their arrogance and authority.

14. They wanted to stay together rather than fill the earth.

15. He opposed it.

16. Man's creative potential used in defiance of God would be a greater problem.

17. Their choices caused them to lose the unity they already had. Their choices led to confusion and division.

18. Personal answers.

19. He told his wife to say she was his sister.

20. He put himself ahead of others, and he lied.

21. A plague occurred.

22. He expected the truth.

23. He asked Abram to take Sarai and get out of there.

24. Abraham committed the same dishonest act as before.

25. (a) Sarah—She lied about having laughed at the prophecy of a son's birth within a year. (b) Isaac—He lied and said his wife was his sister. (c) Jacob—He lied to his father about his identity. (d) Laban—He lied to his nephew, Jacob, about giving him his daughter Rachel. (e) Joseph's brothers—They lied about what happened to their brother.

26. Our actions influence others for good or bad.

## Lesson 4

1. God spoke directly to Moses. God promised blessing for obedience. God gave specific instructions for preparation and procedures of the people before meeting with Him. God warned that people would die if they touched the mountain. The meeting was accompanied by thunder, lightning, thick clouds, and trumpets.

2. God set limits beyond which He did not want the people to go. If they violated those boundaries, there would be consequences.

3. Personal answers.

4. Courts; classrooms.

5. He was asserting His ultimate authority.

6. You would be living by a different moral standard.

7. Friends, cultural standards, other religions.

8. Negative effect if the standards did not match God's standards.

9. (a) Restatement—It tells listeners to turn from "useless things" to "the living God, who made . . . all things." (b) Context—Paul healed a man, and the townspeople concluded that Paul and Barnabas were gods.

10. No.

11. They made an image of a god.

12. They may have been afraid and impatient. They were influenced by the paganism that surrounded them.

13. Man refuses to acknowledge the true God. Man's heart becomes dark. He sees himself as being wise. His thoughts are diminished, becoming futile.

14. It's foolish to worship a man-made god; it has a mouth that can't speak, eyes that can't see, ears that can't hear, a nose that can't smell, hands that can't handle, feet that can't walk.

15. Lustful, immoral activities that are contrary to God's moral standards.

16. He is God. He is Creator. He is Head of the church.

17. Christ is the true God. Keep yourself from idols.

18. Swearing, speaking of God in an irreverent manner.

19. (a) Lead him to disrespect God, to reject His standards. (b) Personal answers.

20. Personal answers.

21. People who do not respect God as the final authority will often take liberties with their ethical standards and will adopt standards contrary to God's standards.

22. (a) Praying—Not recognize the value or power of prayer. Might also become overly casual in communicating with God. (b) Singing—Trivialize worship. (c) Speaking—Not respectfully or accurately representing God. (d) Making promises—People may use the expression "swear to God" and then go back on their word.

23. Everything a believer does is to be done as a representative of God, in the character of Christ.

**Lesson 5**

1. Work and rest.

2. God designed believers for good works.

3. (a) Proverbs 6:6–11—God expects believers to be hard workers, as illustrated by ants. Believers are not to be lazy. (b) Ephesians 6:5–9—Employees are to be as obedient to their employers as they would be to Christ, not doing work just to please men, but doing their work for the Lord. Employers should treat their employees in a godly manner. (c) 2 Thessalonians 3:7–15—Believers should work for their own living and not be a burden to others. They should refrain from being nonworking busybodies. If believers do not follow these guidelines, they should be admonished. (d) 1 Peter 2:18–23—Employees should show respect to employers even when they are harsh.

4. Personal answers.

5. People, cattle, and visitors.

6. (a) Exodus 31:12–17—It was a sign that God was acknowledged as the creator and that God designated Israel as a special people whom He sanctified. (b) Exodus 35:3—Do not kindle a fire in a dwelling. (c) Exodus 16:4–36—Gather extra manna on the sixth day and prepare it. Do not prepare on the Sabbath, but eat. (d) Numbers 28:9, 10—Instruction about burnt offering on the Sabbath. (e) Nehemiah 13:15–21—Wrong to do business on the Sabbath.

7. To give rest.

8. It is not by our works that we are saved, but by God's grace.

9. (a) Exodus 20:12—Children are to honor their parents. (b) Proverbs 4:1–9—A father teaches his children, and the children heed the instruction. (c) Proverbs 31—A mother plays a key role in training her children. (d) Colossians 3:18–21—Husbands are to love their wives, wives are to submit to their husbands, children are to obey their parents, fathers are not to provoke their children.

10. Personal answers.

11. Homicide, abortion, mercy killing, genocide, terrorism, ethnic cleansing.

12. Man is made in the image of God.

13. Hatred leads to murder. It is as though a murder has been committed in a person's mind.

14. Religious, ethnic, marriage, family, political.

15. Love your enemies rather than hate them. Demonstrate kindness to others who do not show kindness to you.

16. Love one another.

17. Personal answers.

**Lesson 6**

1. The law exposes a person as a sinner.

2. Do not be deceived because fornicators, adulterers, homosexuals, and sodomites will not inherit the kingdom of God.

3. (a) Exodus 20:14—Do not commit adultery. (b) Matthew 5:27, 28—Do not lust after a woman in your heart. It is the same as committing adultery. (c) 1 Corinthians 6:12–20—The believer's body is not to be used for sexual immorality. Do not be joined to a harlot. The body is the temple of the Holy Spirit. (d) 1 Corinthians 7:1–5—Marriage can help avoid sexual immorality. A man and woman should give themselves physically to each other. Each has authority over the other's body. (e) 1 Thessalonians 4:1–8—It is God's will that you abstain from sexual immorality. You should know how to control you body in a godly manner. You should not take advantage of another person sexually.

4. Personal answers.

5. (a) Exodus 22:1–15—There are serious consequences for stealing. You are not to take someone else's property or possessions. (b) Leviticus 19:13–15—Do not cheat your neighbor. Pay an employee promptly. Be impartial with the poor and the rich. (c) Leviticus 19:35, 36—Measurements must be accurate. (d) Leviticus 25:35–38—Help a brother who falls into poverty. Do not take advantage of him by charging interest on a loan.

6. Do not steal but work with your hands to make a profit so you can share with those in need.

7. (a) Lumber salesman—Short a customer on board footage. (b) Employer of migrant workers—Do not pay wages promptly. (c) Oil company executive—Overcharge consumers with inflated prices. (d) Farmer—Allow animals to graze on someone else's property. (e) Government contractor—Overcharge for purchased items.

8. Nothing would be safe. People would constantly take from others. It would create anger and revenge. Chaos would ensue.

9. I will not misrepresent my neighbor.

10. Do not lie to one another since you have put off the old man.

11. (a) Courtroom—Justice would not prevail. The wrong person might be found guilty, or the guilty might go free. (b) Job application—A person might put inaccurate information on a résumé. (c) Military intelligence—Information would be inflated for political gains. (d) Newsroom—A story would not be accurately reported. A person's quote might be misrepresented. (f) Historical accounts—History could be rewritten to achieve an ulterior motive.

12. (a) Laban—Laban coveted Jacob's success in business ventures, so he determined to damage Jacob. (b) Jacob's sons—They resented and coveted the favor their father gave Joseph, so they took revenge on him. (c) Saul—He coveted David's success and popularity, and sought to kill David. (d) David—He wanted her, so he arranged to have her husband killed and tried to cover it up. (e) Ahab—Ahab had to have the property belonging to Naboth. Ahab's wife arranged to get the property for Ahab by having Naboth killed.

13. Covetousness is not to be named in the behavior of a believer.

14. A feeling of resentment that someone has more than him. Lust.

15. For a while the coveting can be played out in his mind.

16. He will eventually seek to get what his mind desires. He would craft a scheme to achieve his goal.

17. If you violate one of God's commands, it is as though you are guilty of violating all of them.

18. The law makes everyone guilty. It provides the knowledge of sin.

19. He died in my place when I was ungodly.

20. While I was still a sinner, Christ died for me.

21. You are justified by Christ's blood and saved from wrath through Him.

22. At one time we were enemies; now we are reconciled to God.

23. Death.

24. By grace we are no longer under the penalty of death for our sin. We are justified and now will reign in life.

25. Grace abounds so that now the believer has eternal life.

26. If you will confess with your mouth the Lord Jesus and believe that He is raised from the dead, you will be saved. You will believe unto righteousness.

27. Personal answers.

**Lesson 7**

1. Eight.

2. Don't let corrupt communication come from your mouth; don't demonstrate wrath or malice; don't fellowship with the unfruitful works of darkness.

3.

| Don't | Do |
| --- | --- |
| Make idols | Worship God reverently |
| Covet | Share with others what is yours |
| Commit adultery | Respect and love your spouse |
| Gossip | Speak kindly about others |
| Hate | Love others |
| Be slothful | Work hard |
| Pervert justice | Demonstrate justice |
| Hold a grudge | Forgive |
| Seek revenge | Do kindness to others who wrong you |

4. Personal answers.

5. Love God with all your heart, soul, mind, and strength. Love your neighbor as yourself.

6. A husband is to love his wife as Christ loved the church and as the husband loves his own body. A husband is to dwell with his wife, recognizing that she is a weaker vessel and needs to be treated with understanding and sensitivity.

7. To instruct them, raise them in the nurture and admonition of the Lord, and not provoke them to wrath.

8. To not get involved with a morally loose woman.

9. A family is to care for a parent or grandparent who is widowed.

10. It would be worse than theological infidelity.

11. If the family cannot help, the church is to assist widows who meet the requirements.

12. Anyone with whom we come in contact is our neighbor.

13. Cared for his injuries, transported him, and cared for his lodging and board until he had recovered.

14. Personal answers.

15. Not cheating or stealing. Treating others fairly. Being generous towards others. Paying employees promptly. Fulfilling promises.

16. (a) 1 Timothy 6:1, 2—Honor your employer. Do not take advantage of your employer if he is a believer. (b) Colossians 4:1—Reward your employees fairly for their work. (c) 1 Peter 2:18–23—Submit to your employer even if he is harsh and you have to endure grief and suffering wrongfully.

18. and 19. Personal answers.

20. (a) James 2:1–13—Do not treat people of financial means better than poor people. (b) Revelation 5:8, 9—Treat fellow believers with

respect and love, because believers from every tribe and tongue and nation will be in Heaven together. (c) Genesis 5:1, 2—Man is made in the likeness of God.

21. Personal answers.

22. (a) Matthew 5:43–48—Show kindness to people even when they are unkind. Do good to them and pray for them. (b) Matthew 18:15–17—If an offense has occurred, follow the procedure to confront the person causing the offense. (c) Matthew 18:21–35—Forgive repeatedly. (d) Romans 12:17–21—Do not repay evil with evil. Overcome evil with good. Turn matters for vengeance over to the Lord.

23. He admitted that he was pulled in two ways because of his natures—toward God's righteous way in one direction and toward sin in the other direction.

24. God makes available to us all resources that pertain to life and godliness. He can equip and empower us to live ethically obedient lives.

## Lesson 8
*Suggested answers for Biblical-basis questions:*

3. Exodus 20:15; Matthew 15:19; 19:18; Romans 13:9; 1 Corinthians 6:8–10; Ephesians 4:28; 1 Peter 4:15.

7. Deuteronomy 25:13–16; Proverbs 11:1; 12:22; Luke 6:31; Acts 24:16; Romans 14:12, 13; 2 Corinthians 7:2; Hebrews 13:18.

12. Psalm 15:5; Proverbs 6:30, 31; Ezekiel 22:29; Matthew 6:19, 20; 1 Thessalonians 4:11, 12; 1 Peter 2:12.

16. Genesis 1:26, 27; 5:1, 2; Matthew 28:19, 20; Colossians 3:10, 11; James 2:1–13; Revelation 5:8, 9.

20. Genesis 2:21–25; 39:6–23; Exodus 20:17; 2 Samuel 11; Matthew 5:27–30; 1 Corinthians 7:1–9; Ephesians 5:25–33; 1 Thessalonians 4:1–8.

24. Genesis 7:25–35; Exodus 23:1, 7; Deuteronomy 5:20; Psalm 119:104; Proverbs 12:5; 14:5; 19:5, 9; Mark 7:22.

27. Exodus 23:1; Leviticus 6:2–5; 19:11, 12; Proverbs 3:3; 6:16–19; 12:17–22; 14:5, 8, 25; Ephesians 4:25.

29. Psalm 24:4; 33:4; 51:6; 89:14; Proverbs 1:8–10, 2; Isaiah 33:15, 16; 59:14, 15.

33. Genesis 3:6; Exodus 20:17; Job 31:9–12; Proverbs 6:24, 25; Matthew 5:28; Ephesians 4:22; James 1:14, 15; 1 Peter 2:11; 1 John 2:16, 17.

39. Matthew 18:6, 7, 15–17; Mark 10:13–16.